JUPITER

by L. L. Owens

The Child's World®

Published by The Child's World®
1980 Lookout Drive • Mankato, MN 56003-1705
800-599-READ • www.childsworld.com

ACKNOWLEDGMENTS
The Child's World®: Mary Berendes, Publishing Director
The Design Lab: Design and production
Red Line Editorial: Editorial direction

PHOTO CREDITS
NASA/JPL/University of Arizona/courtesy of nasaimages.org, cover, 1, 25, 32; NASA/
courtesy of nasaimages.org, cover, 1, 3, 6, 12, 14, 18, 20, 23, 28, 31; Paul Cunningham/
AP Images, 5; NASA/courtesy of nasaimages.org/The Design Lab, 6, 7; NASA/JPL/
University of Arizona/courtesy of nasaimages.org/The Design Lab, 9; NASA Jet Propulsion
Laboratory (NASA-JPL), 11; Mikhail Khromov/iStockphoto, 13; Georgios Kollidas/
iStockphoto, 15; NASA/JHU-APL/Southwest Research Institute/courtesy of nasaimages.
org, 17 ; NASA/NSSDC/Catalog of Spaceborne Imaging, 19, 21, 27; NASA/Southwest
Research Institute (Dan Durda)/Johns Hopkins University Applied Physics Laboratory (Ken
Moscati)/courtesy of nasaimages.org, 29

LIBRARY OF CONGRESS CATALOGING-IN-PUBLICATION DATA
Owens, L. L.
  Jupiter / by L.L. Owens.
     p. cm.
  Includes bibliographical references and index.
  ISBN 978-1-60954-382-2 (library bound : alk. paper)
  1. Jupiter (Planet)—Juvenile literature. I. Title.
  QB661.O94 2011
  523.45—dc22
                              2010039959

Printed in the United States of America
Mankato, MN
December, 2010
PA02072

ON THE COVER
Jupiter's colorful layers give the
planet a unique appearance.

Table of Contents

Jupiter and the Solar System

Try looking high in the sky just before sunrise. Do you see a star that looks like a bright white light? That's Jupiter!

Jupiter is one of our space neighbors in the **solar system**. At the center of our solar system is the sun. Planets go around, or **orbit**, the sun.

Jupiter (center) is seen with
Venus (top right) in 2008.

SUN

Mercury

Venus

Earth

Mars

Ceres

Jupiter

Fun Facts

PLANET NUMBER: Jupiter is the fifth planet from the sun.

DISTANCE FROM SUN: 484 million miles (779 million km)

SIZE: Jupiter is the largest planet in our solar system. It is about 279,118 miles (449,197 km) around its middle. That's more than 11 times bigger than Earth's middle!

OUR SOLAR SYSTEM: Our solar system has eight planets and five **dwarf planets**. Pluto used to be called a planet. But in 2006, scientists decided to call it a dwarf planet instead. Scientists hope to discover even more dwarf planets in our solar system!

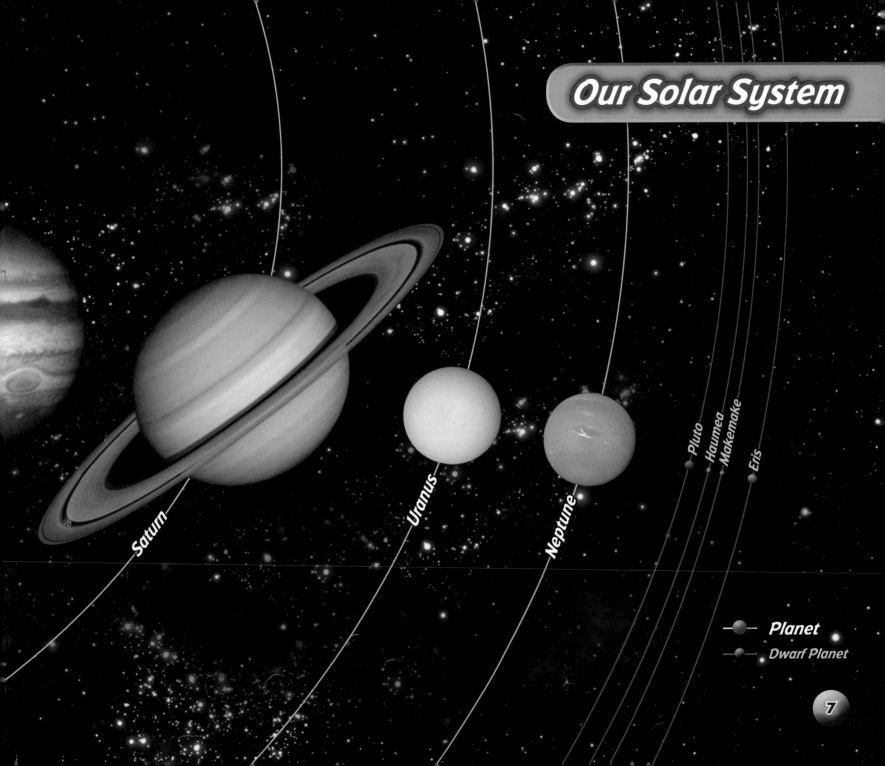

Our Solar System

Saturn

Uranus

Neptune

Pluto
Haumea
Makemake

Eris

Planet

Dwarf Planet

7

While orbiting the sun, a planet spins like a top. Each planet spins, or rotates, on its **axis**. An axis is an imaginary line that runs through a planet from top to bottom. One rotation equals one day. Think of one day on a planet as the time from one sunrise to the next sunrise.

A day on Earth is 24 hours. Jupiter rotates on its axis about once every ten hours. It has the shortest day in the solar system!

An axis runs through the center of a planet. The planet spins on the axis.

One year is the time it takes for a planet to travel around the sun once. A year on Earth is about 365 days. Jupiter travels slowly. It takes Jupiter about 4,333 days to go around the sun—that's almost 12 Earth years.

Jupiter spins quickly but orbits slowly. These nine images of Jupiter were taken as the planet spun.

King of the Planets

More than 2,000 years ago, ancient Romans studied the sky. They **observed** the sun, the moon, and the brightest planets. They named the biggest planet after Jupiter—their king of the gods and lord of the sky.

Jupiter is often called the Giant Planet. More than 1,000 Earths would fit inside it!

The god Jupiter was thought to control weather, such as lightning.

Jupiter's Moons

Some planets have moons that orbit them. Earth has one moon. Jupiter has more than 60! It has the most of all the planets.

From Earth you can see Jupiter's four largest moons. Galileo Galilei discovered them in 1610. He was a famous **astronomer**.

Fun Fact

Jupiter's four largest moons are named Io (EYE-oh), Europa (yu-ROH-pa), Ganymede (GAH-nih-meed), and Callisto (kah-LISS-toe).

Galileo Galilei lived from
1564 to 1642.

An Invisible Force

Gravity is a strong force, but you can't see it. Try jumping in the air. What happens? You come back down to the ground! Gravity is what pulls you down to Earth.

Large objects have stronger gravity. Jupiter has the strongest gravity of all the planets. Objects such as **asteroids** that travel close to Jupiter might get pulled toward the planet. Scientists think Jupiter's strong gravity is why the planet has so many moons.

Strong gravity keeps Jupiter's moons, including Io, Europa, Ganymede, and Callisto, orbiting the planet.

Io   **Europa**   **Ganymede**   **Callisto**

Layers of Gas

Some planets have hard, rocky surfaces. But Jupiter is a **gas** giant. It has no hard surface. Instead, the planet is made of layers of gas and liquid.

Fun Fact

There are two types of planets.

TERRESTRIAL PLANETS (mostly rock) are close to the sun. They are: Mercury, Venus, Earth, and Mars.

GAS GIANTS (mostly gas and liquid) are farther from the sun. They are: Jupiter, Saturn, Uranus, and Neptune.

Jupiter has four very faint rings. The white line shows where one ring is located.

A Swirling Atmosphere

In space, Jupiter looks as if it is covered in swirling bands of orange, brown, red, yellow, and white. **Chemicals** in Jupiter's clouds create these colorful layers.

An **atmosphere** is the layer of gas around a planet. Earth's atmosphere is the air we breathe. Because Jupiter is a gas giant, you could say that the planet is almost all atmosphere.

Fun Fact

Jupiter is made of the same gases as a star. But even though Jupiter is huge, it is not big enough to be called a star.

The colors in this image have been brightened to show Jupiter's swirling clouds.

All life as we know it needs water. Scientists are looking for water on other planets to see if life exists on them. Jupiter has some **water vapor** in its atmosphere.

But scientists have found no traces of life on Jupiter. Remember, there is no solid surface. Any living thing on the planet would need to survive in Jupiter's atmosphere.

An artist created this image of the *Galileo* spacecraft arriving at Jupiter in 1995 to study the planet.

A Toxic Planet

Even if you could walk on Jupiter, you would not be able to breathe. Jupiter's thick cloud layers are **toxic**.

Gases on Jupiter smell like rotten eggs. And its temperatures change a lot. Cloud temperatures reach −230°F (−145°C). But the center of Jupiter—its core—is even hotter than the surface of the sun.

In this image, white areas show storms of gas that are high in Jupiter's thick atmosphere.

Jupiter's high winds keep the clouds moving and storms forming. Astronomers with early **telescopes** noticed the Great Red Spot on Jupiter about 400 years ago. It is a giant storm. Its winds rage at speeds up to 400 miles per hour (645 km/h). That is twice the speed of Earth's most dangerous hurricanes!

Scientists say the Great Red Spot storm is slowly getting smaller. They think the storm will end someday.

This image shows the Great Red Spot in 1979.

27

Exploring the Planet

The NASA spacecraft *Juno* is scheduled to reach Jupiter in 2016. Scientists have put a special shield around its electronic parts. They don't want *Juno* to melt or explode.

Scientists hope *Juno* will discover how much water is in Jupiter's atmosphere. This can help them learn how the gas giant was formed. They might discover what's underneath all those layers of gas!

Fun Fact

NASA stands for the National Aeronautics and Space Administration. It is a US agency that studies space and the planets.

An artist shows the *New Horizons* spacecraft as it flew by Jupiter in 2007 on its way to the outer parts of our solar system.

GLOSSARY

asteroids (ASS-tuh-roidz): Asteroids are rocks that orbit the sun. Asteroids that pass by Jupiter might be pulled in by Jupiter's gravity.

astronomer (uh-STRON-uh-mer): An astronomer is a person who studies planets, stars, or moons. Galileo Galilei was a famous astronomer who discovered Jupiter's four largest moons.

atmosphere (AT-muhss-fihr): An atmosphere is the mixture of gases around a planet or a star. Jupiter's atmosphere has thick, swirling clouds.

axis (AK-siss): An axis is an imaginary line that runs through the center of a planet or a moon. Jupiter rotates on its axis.

chemicals (KEM-uh-kuhlz): Chemicals are substances used in chemistry that are sometimes found in the atmospheres of planets. Chemicals in Jupiter's atmosphere make colorful cloud layers.

dwarf planets (DWORF PLAN-itz): Dwarf planets are round bodies in space that orbit the sun, are not moons, and are not large enough to clear away their paths around the sun. Dwarf planets often have similar objects that orbit near them.

gas (GASS): A gas is a substance that moves around freely and can spread out. Jupiter is made of layers of gas and liquid.

gravity (GRAV-uh-tee): Gravity is a force that pulls objects toward each other. Gravity pulls Jupiter along its path around the sun.

observed (uhb-ZURVD): If something is observed, it is watched and studied closely. Ancient Romans observed the night sky.

orbit (OR-bit): To orbit is to travel around another body in space, often in an oval path. Planets orbit the sun.

solar system (SOH-lur SISS-tum): Our solar system is made up of the sun, eight planets and their moons, and smaller bodies that orbit the sun. Jupiter is the fifth planet from the sun in our solar system.

telescopes (TEL-uh-skohps): Telescopes are tools for making faraway objects appear closer. Scientists observe Jupiter using telescopes on Earth and in space.

toxic (TOK-sik): To be toxic is to be poisonous. Jupiter's thick clouds are toxic.

water vapor (WAW-tur VAY-pur): Water vapor is water in the air as gas. Jupiter's atmosphere has some water vapor.

FURTHER INFORMATION

BOOKS

Elkins-Tanton, Linda. *Jupiter and Saturn*. New York: Facts on File, 2010.

Landau, Elaine. *Jupiter*. New York: Children's Press, 2008.

Trammel, Howard K. *The Solar System*. New York: Children's Press, 2010.

WEB SITES

Visit our Web site for links about Jupiter: **childsworld.com/links**

Note to Parents, Teachers, and Librarians: We routinely verify our Web links to make sure they are safe and active sites. So encourage your readers to check them out!

INDEX

ABOUT THE AUTHOR

L. L. Owens has been writing books for children since 1998. She writes both fiction and nonfiction and especially loves helping kids explore the world around them.